Bob at Bat

by Nicole Michael
illustrated by Len Epstein

Core Decodable 17

McGraw Hill Education

Bothell, WA • Chicago, IL • Columbus, OH • New York, NY

MHEonline.com

Send all inquiries to:
McGraw-Hill Education
8787 Orion Place
Columbus, OH 43240

ISBN: 978-0-02-144915-6
MHID: 0-02-144915-5

Printed in Canada.

9 10 11 12 KOD 24

Bob is at bat.

Bob stamps a bit.

Bob taps a bat.

Bob can stand and nod.

Bob bats. Bam!
Bob has a hit!

Bob pants and pants.